My Father's Pigs

Roland Leach

My Father's Pigs

PICARO PRESS

Acknowledgements

I am grateful to the editors of the following publications, in which earlier versions of these poems first appeared: *Antipodes* (ed. Margaret Bradstock), *Blue Dog*, *Conversations* (Australian National University), *Ekleksographia*, *Famous Reporter*, *HEAT*, *Indigo*, *ISLAND*, *Overland*, *Scatterlings of Empire* (Journal of Australian Studies, UQP), *stylus*, *Tamba*, *The Night Road* (ed. Philip Salom & Jill Jones, Hunter Writers' Centre), *Westerly*

My Father's Pigs
ISBN 978 1 921691 29 4
Copyright © text Roland Leach 2011
Cover image: http://upload.wikimedia.org/wikipedia/commons/e/
e5/StateLibQld_1_239484_Sawmill_at_Sandy_Creek.jpg

This edition published 2017 by
Picaro Press – an imprint of
GINNINDERRA PRESS
PO Box 3461 Port Adelaide 5015 Australia
www.ginninderrapress.com.au

Contents

My Father's Pigs	7
Photograph	8
Falling	9
The Swell Sonnets	14
Flesh Made Doubt	18
Into the Desert	19
Pushing	20
Charles Darwin & Emma Wedgwood: Three Poems	21
Wilderness	24
set:tle:ment	26
Middle East Sonnets	27
Medewi Fishing	30
Goat Track	31
Body Surfing	32
Stones	33
Bodies	37
Leaving her that morning	38
Small Murders	39
Behind the Gardens	40
For my Mother	42
Surgeons and Anaesthetists	43
The Sea Home	44
Galapagos	46
On Being Fifty	47
Altitude	48
Rakata Spider	49
From The Book of Water	50
Argo	56
Love	57
Between the Reefs	58
Cat	60

My Father's Pigs

My father tells me
that he has just come back
from killing pigs at old Vern Brewster's place,
bleed like bejesus,
and he looks at his hands
surprised they are so clean.

My sister had encouraged us
to tell him, No Dad, you're in a nursing home,
but that's long ago
and we know he would have preferred
to have died in a bar-room brawl,
been abandoned in the forest
than this soft finish.

So I ask how many pigs Vern has?
their weight, ask if it's true
that they will kill you if you finish up
arse-over-tit in the dirt?
and he brightens up,
as happy as a pig in shit,
as if no one has asked a sensible question
in the last month.

Photograph

We have kept photographs. Derelict
timber mill outside Cowaramup.
Sunburnt and half-drunk in an old hut.
We have the photographs. The camera
has caught us young: in the millshed giving
obscene gestures, pretending to have two
fingers amongst the rusted ruins
of circular saws. We have a photograph.
All of us. The five of us. All there.
An old winch around our necks like a shark hook.
Like a steel noose. Wearing Indian shirts
and long hair. We have photographs. Like a hook.
The mill. The winch. Our necks. Us five.
The photographs have caught us all alive.

Falling

1

My mother always
had dreams of
falling

she fell
each night
from the same lighthouse

the lighthouse
a thin white babel
now silent

always a still blue day
and her
falling

dressed like her
Irish mother
the white petticoat

ballooning
around her head
like white folded wings.

2

There is an art to falling:
avoid hard surfaces
but surfaces can be deceptive
even deep water will break your neck

When falling from high altitudes
it is possible
if you dare to have the imagination
to believe it is simply flight.

3

My grandmother never believed
you should fall in love
in her diaries she mused
on the phrase falling in love

and imagined parachutists
falling from World War I planes
always into enemy territory

silken cords around her limp neck
limbs tangled in high trees
like pale broken trunks

she was a woman
who knew about surfaces
knew the art of surfacing

all life's lessons were useless
if you couldn't master this
though she would never use the word.

4

She lived in a time
where they used phrases like
the cream always rises to the top
one should keep to one's station in life

and it was not so much falling
as staying where you were
though she often believed
someone had sewn stones
into the seams of her pockets.

5

She fell all the way to Australia,
even worse, Perth,
arriving in her exile
wearing arrogant black
and taking to the streets with a swagger

believing one could be free
at the end of the world,
she grew careless and didn't care

and when they called her a fallen woman
she laughed, showing them her body
immaculate and unbruised,
free of any injury that one might expect from a fall.

6

Is there a difference between
a fallen angel & a falling angel,
how far do they fall
before they are fallen?

7

Before my mother married
she grew a vision of the future:
there was a neat house with high ceilings,
a large mantelpiece with photographs
of the children as they were growing.

She imagined herself changing them every few years,
the frames would be silver embossed
and they would be slightly turned
to the centre of the mantelpiece
and her achievement would be visible
every time she walked into the room.

In the garden there had to be roses,
red and white roses,
and a pathway that ran straight
from the gate to the porch steps

and it was only in dreams
that her own mother ever
appeared
falling from the sky,

her white petticoats
ballooning over her head
so her face remained
forever veiled.

The Swell Sonnets

1

The swell. On the night beach. As if some titan
is thrashing a leviathan against the sand dunes.
The thrash and thump, the spray of ocean caught
in crevices of wind. The swell. Leviathan ocean.
Infatuation of morning where the world
changes overnight. The blue backdrop
to the coast road had come alive. The magic
of a child's story. Sea creatures on the page
prowling mountains, savannah. Riding waves.
The swell birthed by storm on the edge of another continent.
Energy to light a country for a hundred years.
Weed and bluebottles. Picassos on sand. The swell.
Casting out eyes, trawling in a narrative. Wet titans,
beached leviathans. The thrash and tumble. The sound of homage.

2

Casting out eyes trawling in a narrative. Lost perhaps
for hundreds of years. The great sailing ships when they were
small. Meagre boats. Takes brave men to leave land.
Years before a compass. Odysseus. Listening to a night beach.
The spell of swell. The alluring shore. Casting out lines
for night tailor. When my father walked the shore
one hand on the rod, one on nylon line. Casting.
Out lives. Together. The safety of land. Forcing
the ocean back. Back within pages. The story
we told. The narrative we learnt about our. Selves.
Throwing away the fish-heads of night. Walking
back to the lights on the hill. The safety of light.
When my father opened doors he always looked behind.
As if he heard the ocean. Wet and dripping wanting the key.

3

They are surfing the Bay, off the back reef.
The sound of wave is thunder. It's the sound
of towers falling. Great walls keeping out hordes.
Collapsing. A surfer escapes the white rain of wave.
Hostage to a watery fiefdom. Towers falling.
His starched blonde hair, curly & long almost untouched.
I am twelve years old. Will remember this day of art.
This ocean. The storms that stir its ocean heart, a muscle-flexed
swell that sculpts waves. The art of waves. Its breath.
A white trail of board that carves vertical strokes
spins down onto blue canvas that rolls into. Itself.
We wait for storms. Wait for an offshore wind
to coat the swell with a thin cover of glass.
The sun on our backs. The slash of white paint.

4

Offshore easterly pushing any swell out
to sea, to a far continent. I have my goggles on
swimming along the back of reef seeing the old
red-lips, slow & stern, silver bream slanted on an angle
eating weed, angelfish in their startled stripes beneath the reef.
Later there will be tailor. Pugilist-faced, lean and silver blue.
I am no longer an adolescent. It's come
quite late. The colour of sky reminded me.
I was always younger in summer. There is a fluidity
I am trying to gather as I dive to the bottom.
Lean and silver blue. Stripped of all brightness.
Nothing superfluous. You can be that way in the ocean.
Stripping back the seamless pulse of planet, its quietness.
As if rising to the surface and taking your next breath mattered.

Flesh Made Doubt

1

It was Gabriel and a beating of wings
come to erase a debt
who seeded the child-woman with words

she is small-breasted & immaculate
drawing water with a pitcher
when the angel appears

inside her is a kernel
a space sealed from noise
that is immune to the world

and she answers yes
making word flesh

2

Later it is the answer yes,
her acquiescence to a beating of wings,
a voice that may have been imagined,
that bothers her.

Into the Desert

Christ went into the desert. The solitude
of stone, a cold night sky. Gods only
inhabit the desert and sea. You won't
find them in cities and towns. They don't
like crowds, prefer moonlight on water,
the sands cooling down. A place where
it is one-on-one
        face to face
choose your weapon
Christ went into the desert armed with silence.
Prepared to face light and darkness
in a night sky. Feeding himself a vision
before returning to Galilee.
As thin as hunger. As wild as love.

Pushing

You can only know the world by pushing
against it. Feet placed flat, leaning into it,
just a touch at first so it knows you exist.
Despite what you hear it is not indifferent,
just needs you to make this first act of touch.
It may still slip you into a crevasse
wipe you out with a rare virus,
or may smile allowing you to know
its contours, hidden clefts, back rows.

Do not take it personally.
Just take these as lessons in the world
where you learn what you will put up with,
and if the moon is sufficiently inclined,
perhaps discover something extinct alive
which refuses to bend with the wind,
to nod when spoken to,
or be pleased with the sheer gratitude
of being left alone.

Charles Darwin & Emma Wedgwood: Three Poems

1. Darwin 1838

He has inside his head the first spark, a burning,
that will set fires, worse than any Inquisitor's flames.
At times he sees himself as a pyromaniac, lightning emanating
from his fingertips, burning the City of God. He knows it
and doesn't know it, unsure and wanting to keep God
on his side, but behind this affable man, so courteous
and agreeable, a man who almost wore a collar, is a secret.
He imagines it as a white patch, petal-shaped, that has lodged
in the right sphere of his brain, that greys sometimes to doubt,
but always reappears. At the moment it has darkened and
is dragging him down, doubling him over in stomach pains,
but he never wishes it to leave.

It sets him apart, it is a secret after all, and he is keeping it
to himself. There are the evenings at the Athenaeum
that he wouldn't give up: the soft sinking into leather,
the port & cigars, the admiration of powerful men.
But inside his head a light is dawning, like some God
has decreed the beginning of a world, and he feels it descending
to a common ancestor and further back still. For the moment
he cannot speculate on it, his stomach pains erupt when he
imagines the consequences. Still not established or married
he knows this could so easily break him. He has within
that white petal, that fire, something worse than any
Dissenter has proposed and he has seen enough of them
fall from the graces. He will take his time, never imagines
himself a genius, but he has the patience of a born observer,
and has no peer. It is this gift, green and like the side of a mountain,
that he intends to cling till the moment is right.

2. Darwin's Proposal

'As for a wife, that most interesting specimen in the whole series of vertebrate animals, Providence only knows whether I shall ever capture one or be able to feed her if caught.' – Charles Darwin

Getting close to thirty
he thought of marriage
and made a for and against column
on a blue scrap of paper.

There were shackles that he may not be able to bear:
to travel where you will,
nights out and clever talk,
and of course the terrible expense
and anxiety of children.

What was a man without wife & children?
Your own blood that would live on
and be a second life as he called it,
a wife for companionship, a friend in old age,
an object to be beloved and played with,
much better than a dog, and imagine a nice warm home
with the fire aglow and a soft wife on the sofa,
the charms of music & female chit-chat,
all good for the health, unlike growing old alone,
a dribbling fool leaving only a set of old books,
yes he must marry and went and saw Emma Wedgwood.

3. Eternity

'I am the vine, ye are the branches... If a man abide not in me, he is cast forth as a branch and is withered; and men gather them, and cast them into fire, and they are burned.' – John, XIII

Emma had sent her fiancee away to read
the end of John, chapter thirteen,
of Christ telling the disciples of the place
he had prepared for the faithful.

She intends to be united with her dead sister,
imagines heaven with clear skies
and roses blooming all year round,
and wishes Charles to be there too
but since hearing an outline of his work
she has mourned the loss of his soul.
She fears the fires of hell for him
and knows there can be no eternity for them.

He thinks of fire & heat in geological terms,
and has seen it erupt at the end of the earth.
He doesn't fear it in the green country of Down.
As for vines & branches he has been working on his own,
humans appear at the far tip and it is the tracing back
to the vine that he has set his lifework.
It is this descent that seems like eternity.

Wilderness

1

The word panic
once meant to feel the fear
of wilderness

imagining the god, Pan,
with his untamed tastes
appearing from the smiling

dark of forest
before you could
scream.

A forest of fairy tales,
a place of witches & wolves –
creatures who don't obey

2

straight lines or need light
to know who they are.

So the trees were cut
and canopies collapsed
allowing light to dissolve the dark
to create settlements,

which is another word:
to feel at ease, to stay in one place,
not to venture out

to know that things
will not/can not
appear suddenly at your door

with the wet smell
of undergrowth in its pores

3

or the long scrape
of claw at the wooden door.

And so it was from the beginning
that the wilderness
was a sentence,
a punishment for transgressors,

and the word 'wilderness'
from will – to be wilful, uncontrolled –

was a place where they were sent
beyond the borders:
the exile of sinners,
wild men who found frontiers,

though it was only those
who got lost in the forest
who learnt who they were,
learnt that the wilderness
was not separate.

set:tle:ment

Settlement. To settle. To allow to set.
Harden and fix. Like glue or old age.
To have settlements you need to demarcate.
Set boundaries, map in borders, mark out
land between civilisation and wilderness.
Between the civil and the wild. It suits
a colonial mind, that finds emptiness
in abundance. It might need flags and guns.
Most probably, God. A belief in permanence.
That timber and stone, steel and roads, will last.
Can make the man. Make the world.
With its safety in straight lines, its walls, walls,
holding back the panic of darkness
that lies outside in all its wild fecundity.

Middle East Sonnets

1. Babel

He never intended to give them words,
knew the fecund rubbing of syllable
on syllable led to riotous talk,
and once spoken were stone temples,
were ropes that held ramparts across rivers,
were nails that joined planks, broke through waves.
So when Nimrod erected his ziggurat
built of burnt brick and cemented clay
it seemed like a missile aimed at him.
He sent down winds from a dozen lands,
filled with mountain echoes, voices of birds
and storms, the sounds of water on rock
and let them fill their mouths till their words
separated them, thick and stone as walls.

2. Gaza 2009

In the land of the first written word
they are forging a new cuneiform. In this
stony land, in empty houses, on walls,
soldiers graffiti vigilante policy:
Arabs need 2 die!!
Make war not peace!
Gaza here we are!
There are drawings, malevolent as prophecy:
Soldiers pissing on toppled muezzin towers.
A gravestone: Arabs 1948–2009.
In this land of walls walls walls they intrude
into the intimacy of rooms. Graffiti is not enough.
The shelling is not enough. Soldiers drop bags of scat.
Leave their scent like great desert cats.

3. Kites

They are flying kites at Beit Lahiya.
Children with kites, women in black burkas.
Attached to the sky. On the beach at Beit
Lahiya where buildings expose their skeletons,
the kites are coloured confetti, they are splashes of paint.
Lifting with the wind, defying gravity.
They are held by blood. Months ago there were
only stray gunmen in alleys. People pleading
for blood. You need wind to defy gravity.
Things fall. It is a law of nature. Bombs
fall. Missiles rise and fall. Buildings expose
their skeletons. It is a law of nature.
On a beach in Gaza with homemade kites
children, women, men, make peace with the sky.

Medewi Fishing

To catch a fish. You need a boat carved from
cassia wood. Nets draped like a bride's veil
from bow side. To have nets you need a boss.
To catch a fish. You set out by moon. Dropping
over the fragile hair of net. Till snapper
and barracuda. Grapple and bundle
themselves into soft drownings. To catch a wife
you need many fish. In the morning the boats
return. Small viking boats. Built of cassia.
The fragile veil of net. You need more fish
for children. You pay the boss fish. Grappling
in the net. The surfacing. The coming home.
To your wife and children with fishloads.
Price of morning on Medewi Bay.

Goat Track

At the end of a goat track along a cliff.
Down steps worn into rocks. Onto a small
white beach. Is Ketut and his outrigger.
To take us to the reefs. To take us to
a white scar of hollowing waves curved
by coral. At the other end of the goat
track is his hut, wife and six year old child.
Inside this man is a belief in all around him:
the shape of the hull, the boat's displacement
of water, his wife and daughter, prospects
of owning land. He likes the surfers he takes
to the reef. Mostly men from a dozen countries
who extravagantly travel thousands
of miles to surf waves for no other reason
than they can. To travel from other worlds to spend
Ketut's year's earnings for a week on this island,
to fit their bodies into the shape of waves.

Body Surfing

You must position your body parallel
to the wave, almost out of the water,
arm straight, palm cupped upward,
elbow a rudder that locks you in.
Then wait as the swell suddenly lifts,
born from a shift in depth,
a gradient pull that steeps the face
for the physics of tubes to be shaped
from the lazy sloping movement of sea.
All so you can be here this day
sliding your body into the arching,
aching body of wave as it lifts vertically.

Stones

i.m. Father John Hawes

(Father Hawes arrived in Geraldton in 1913, in charge of the largest diocese in the world, though with few parishioners. He was an acclaimed architect who designed many churches. He returned to Cat Island in the Caribbean in his later years, dying a hermit.)

1

Emptiness is only space
waiting to be filled
and as a man of God and architect
he knew one started with stone.

So when he looked into a continent
from its western edge,
he imagined churches
carved from white stone
hearing them filled with voices.

2

You need to empty yourself
before you can know God,
a series of unlearnings,
the clearing away of debris.

An excavation
those first churchmen knew,
building great cathedrals full of space
rising to high pitched roofs
where people could spool out
strings of self while still seated.

3

In the tiny town of Mullewa
he built Our Lady of Mount Carmel
with his own hands

mixing up the mortar
carrying each stone up ramps
piling stone
        on stone
smoothing away the edges
till they fitted side by side
as if work was a sacred act.

4

It is the solitude of stone
its cold warmth
the stillness within

that encourage
        those willing to find belief
to feel that first otherness
the numinous presence
that sculpts angel's wings
from shapeless stone.

5

I sometimes think that the stones
        are a part of me
each stone, each piece, like a hieroglyph
as if the Rosetta Stone had been found again
        and each stone
as it is placed onto stone
builds another piece of me
giving me the language to read myself.

6

He liked that stones
                came from earth
pressured together for a million years
so that parts once separate & fragile
were now indistinguishable.

There was an equality in stone
a socialism in their origins
that did not need fossil to find narrative
the fable was always within.

7

There were things he would always love:
a cup of tea at first light
a dog that was always at his feet
riding a winner at a country racetrack

and then the letting go:
the small isle in the caribbean
where a cave in the side of hill
waited his solitude
for him to imagine himself into
silence stone dust

Bodies

When summer came we took off our clothes.
We were not conscious of the body's miracle,
the marvels it could perform. We threw off
our clothes as if they were crowskin.
Summer turned our skins brown, bleached our hair.
We leapt into the ocean, flew across waves,
dived beneath reefs. Bodies were what we woke to.
They were careless and impulsive, attracted
to danger, attracted to other bodies.
There was bruising but the healing quick.
At the end of summer our parents gave back
our clothes in a box. Later when the winds
turned cold south we wore jumpers, kept inside.
Our first glimpse of mortality, the terrible longing for days to pass.

Leaving her that morning

he had walked down to the beach

watching fishermen with their rods
like diviners feeling the nuances of sea

seeing Picassos in the strangle of weed
wide-hipped women as Modiglianis

and with the touch of easterly at his back
he had looked out at Rottnest

which was no longer an island
but a mirage of low cloud

that had earthed itself miraculously
into the body of another

Small Murders

I attempt not to kill
but cannot forgive ants,
their quickness to sense weakness,
their merciless efficiency.
I have given up pogroms
on spiders, moth larvae, even cockroaches,
have persuaded my wife against her genocide
of caterpillars in autumn lilac trees,
but I cannot forgive ants
for their tireless industry and blind allegiance,
for the way they appear from cracks
to latch onto geckos I have saved from the pool,
stuck so tight you almost have to amputate
to free the gecko's limb.

I have been known to pour boiling water
on their sand mounds that appear
in the brick paving after days of dry,
and imagine a reincarnated life
where karma situates me on the leeside
of a volcanic mountain as it flows lava,
red, sulphurous and boiling.

Behind the Gardens

Even if you stepped beyond
the sheltered gardens
the wrought iron gates

there is only
the soft shade
of peppermint trees

where the world seems

Down the streets
the children play
as safe as a cry

the doors are never locked
dogs don't need to growl
neighbours smile across fences

at the shopping centre
fashionable mothers gently
glide their trolleys

down wide aisles
and the world is edible
on neat counters & freezers

All their daughters
grow beautiful
with private school smiles

and boys learn to be
barristers & surgeons
like father & grandfather

and the world seems

One morning
very quietly
two young girls with everything

hanged themselves
from a tree in a vacant block
worth two million dollars

soft as a cry

For my Mother

My father's muscles were earned from decades
lifting timber onto the back of trucks.
When he flexed his arms they rose like
a great swell over deep water,
not threatening till it closed on shore,
which was often the local bar
where he drank and had fights,
but on growing old
he became sentimental and died.
My mother is much tougher,
she's over eighty and hasn't been to a doctor
since her last childbirth,
puts her shoulder into moving wardrobes
and drags back her german shepherd
as if wrestling a lover when he tries going over the fence.

She refuses to die.
Standing at the flywire door armed with her broom,
ready to fight death when she hears the click of the gate.

Surgeons and Anaesthetists

Surgeons are serious people. They need
to be with their arsenal of weaponry.
They reconnoitre the landscape of skin
to incise. The thin muslin peeling back
like chicken skin. Anaesthetists are allowed
a sense of humour, they administer oblivion.
A netherworld lightness as the surgeon bloodies
his hands. They are like deities. Mars
and Morphia in unison. One must wield
sharpened edges while the other brings sleep.
The surgeon at the centre of the sun,
the anaesthetist sitting quietly
like a mother as the earth falls away.
The drip in your arm her warm hand.

The Sea Home

1

It was a long trip home. Cursed winds.
Too many enemies had been made.
It was a long trip, a long curse. Needing to catch
a wily god on a sacred beach to give
us a wind home. Our men hid greased
and stinking beneath skins of seals just slaughtered.
Waiting. For this god, this shape-shifter.
To return to his beloved seals on a sacred
beach. It was a long wait. A beach now
cursed with slaughter. They tried netting this
shape-shifter, but into a great cat he became.
Agile and cunning. Into a serpent.
A panther. Before dissembling to running
water. Before tricked into giving up his prophecy.

2

After all the slaughters. Ten years of war.
The infatuation of princes. Sacrifice
of daughters for wind. The long trip to slaughter.
Young boys thrown from walls. Women sold.
Many enemies had been made. Mothers
and sons. Wives and husbands. The anger
of gods shipwrecking men. So much depended
on wind. The trip home. Long bows bent back.
After all this it would be this day on the
sacred beach. The smell of greased men
with nets. A clumsy husband who was king.
It would be this memory of a god
as running water. Dissembled and fluid.
That made her imagine a self she could live with.

Galapagos

Despite all the longings
the yearnings to be so much more

floating in an old crater
that was a volcano 4 million years ago

it is enough
to be just a higher order mammal

where islands are born
mountains worn back to the water's edge

where creatures crawl from the sea
and grow wings,

it is enough
beneath a sky that remains prehistoric

to hear the great batwings of frigate birds
hover in the sky.

On Being Fifty

I rang a friend on his fiftieth
to tell him not to do anything foolish,
despite there being only decay, decrepitude and death left,
that the body would now quickly falter & fail,
and hoped he wasn't still having sex.
He might find that his jokes were no longer amusing,
that the hard cynic self within had only been a phase,
certainly a long and extended one, but it would pass,
but in his case the possibility of god would not increase.
Having lost all his hair early
at least one humiliation had been spared,
his hirsute body covering was something else.
There is a danger of hugging cats for longer
than would be respectable for a younger man,
buying a car that people would want to touch,
perusing the papers for ocean cruises.
His politics would be right wing
though there was no change there.
Death will appear in unlikely places,
and he will be aware of things dark & undetectable within
that could go off as suddenly as a single-bullet assassin.

I hoped he still believed that life was a narrow rip
sweeping him out to sea,
and was still cocksure as hell that he could swim
across the current anytime he pleased.

Altitude

Faith has more to do
with altitude than attitude.
On the ridge above Machu Picchu
the cadences of the body stills,
each breath its own beautitude.
and our agnostic selves fall away
like packsaddles
and we can imagine Incan priests
searching omens in the constant shifts of light,
divining truths from rumours of stone on stone.

Rakata Spider

The first thing that appeared
after krakatau scorched itself
back to cauterised rock
was a tiny spider,
it is said it must have floated
on thermals from a nearby island
landing like a parachutist
at the beginning of the earth.

I do not know if spiders have psyches,
how it would have fed
but given that it survived
must have thought itself
a survivor of holocaust.

Thirty thousand died in tidal waves
on the islands of Indonesia,
death appearing as a blue swell
littered in pumice & debris three palm trees high,
the sky did not clear for two years
and krakatau was heard
as far away as Perth.

The spider knew nothing of this;
that it had been named the rakata spider
after the famous island excluding its end letters,
only knew it could thread silk
billowing it up into the winds
managing to fly without wings
and amazed at its one trick
may have thought it the reason
the earth was created.

From The Book of Water

(The book was recovered on one of the northern continents, originating probably in the early 21st century)

1

The Book of Water is a serious & ancient work,
a religious exegesis that speaks of creation,
of how all life came from water,
its first divisions,
of multiplications exponential
till all the seas steamed with life.
We are the result of all this,
though perhaps not its end.

(Turn the pages and the paper
moistens under your touch
read of how its speaks of love
as a willingness to become:
this is godness,
god is love,
and a calmness descends.)

It tells that to love another
is to lose all cynicism,
it is a belief that drags you back from darkness,
all things will then matter,
this is love this is god   god is love
thus spoke the prophet Clare,
and you feel the radiance of light.

All is metaphor is the central tenet
in The Book of Water
and we must learn their poetics
is its message.

2

To water
where the book begins
returns to
        and ends

it is the life force
and again we must shrug off
old associations

it is the essence
(the thing all philosophers, alchemists, priests,
scientists and others have fought over)

its lesson is fluidity
you must enter the water
and learn weightlessness
slipping free the gravity of land
letting the universe fill you

3

Like most books found on the planet
it is a quest narrative.
Its hero seeks the stillness
that has been lost
so long ago
that its memory is myth.

Some speak of it as an extinct creature,
others know it lies buried in consciousness,
most have lost all trace,
replacing it with the works of man,
its manifestations in the riches
made from their hands & intellect,
the things you can hang from necks,
wear on fingers,
exhibit so others can measure you,

and it is in their theories,
works of intellect,
erudite explanations of the workings
of the universe,
the everything that explains all
in simple logic & equations,
that the hero sets out to destroy.

He must journey over water
then beneath it.

It is to drowning men and women
that he speaks,
knowing they will hear.

Eighty days he spends alone at sea
living only on water,
as lean as grief,
fighting his hunger
with visions

surviving storms
where waves tower above
like awashed skyscrapers

always watching with calm
not fearing death by water
till a wave hits his craft leeside
and driven to the bottom
he rises again and comes to shore
to tell his stories
of weightlessness fluidity
it is the fish he takes as his symbol
he brings a way of breathing
in another element.

4

The later parts of The Book of Water
are believed to be a satire
of the great land power of the time.
It is a fragmented & elliptical work
where the name of the country shifts and slides
– new calimbus, babellonia, orika –
though it is the one and same nation.

The nation of new calimbus
tricks all into believing its goodness,
it gives and gives,
marketable gifts that says you can be like us,
it is assumed all want shiny gifts,
they smile and have the words of forgiveness,
speak of freedom & liberty,
then slides the other hand
out of the silk glove puppet
to calculate and push buttons,
then slips it back,
a sleight of hand that smiles.

    the night sky full of fire
the eyeless strips   mountains blown to ground
the desert caught fire the jungle caught fire
the concrete caught fire caught fire caught fire

They claim their element is water,
say their prophet is the one who surfaces,
yet their hands are dark with burns,

their ancient craft is words,
upgraded on silicon chip on black type,
downloaded exploded into the faces of their believers
and convince black is white.

They take water
and dam it into slick waterways,
call it the sea,
and have all marvel at its artifice,

(while the rest of the land
is flooded or drained
there are no voices
no words
there is silence)

using water
to fit the lie of the vessel.

So speaketh the prophet,
Marijah of the desert,
who knew that all water
is sacred.

Argo

The Argo is rotting on Corinth Beach,
the timbers lifting like waves, rising like asps,
the heroes have departed,
the women abandoned.

It is time to take stock
of shifting loyalties and betrayals,
admit we have been fleeced.

The great have declared themselves deities,
dividing up the loot in daylight on the streets,
as if it is the will of the gods
and we may have once agreed
acquiesced to the logic of the world,

but it is time to reassess,
find our own boat-builders perhaps
or dare to imagine
that we no longer need
great men on the prows.

The rotting plank is about to fall.

Love

Love is a territory we map with little skill.
We imagine it a place at journey's end,
all the fated roads, even mistook bends
will deliver us always high on a hill,
and we, like conquistadors, appraise our ground.
It is more a place a few stumble upon,
though they will still persist with narratives
of fate, kindred spirits and a madness.

Between the Reefs

i.m. Pat

Can't freestyle because of a motorbike accident after the war,
so I backstroke – like an old windmill, the type that would
drag its arm through the water to move a grinder inside,
from North Cott to Cott, reef to reef,
allowing this old body a bit of time in the sun.
Others watch the water beneath,
silver bream lounging off beds of weed
cod darting in & out of reef, but I use the sky to navigate.
Set my eye up above and for a half-hour
I am lost to anything that isn't above me.
Moving, stroke after stroke, arms straight back
though they splay to the side, dragging the water
to the side of me, that big blue dome above,
as if I was back in the cockpit of a war Spitfire,
but now I can just lay back, head lolling backwards:
a mediation between sea & sky,
with me the navigator between reefs,
the mediator, the meditator between earth & all that is above.

They use to say that I was crazy swimming so far out
but I learnt all I needed to know about fear in the war.
Worked wireless & radio in the RAAF,
right up the front of the plane,
saw the blood spray on the windscreen,
saw the numbers drop in the huts,
the new recruits appearing.

You would freeze then start to shake
before every mission.
Steel yourself men, the commander would say,
so we did till we could feel nothing else,
as if we had been blacksmiths tempering large plates
that would slide in nice and tight up our backbones.

They tell me I'm a lucky bastard.
Escaped death more times than old Methuselah
or was he just plain old?
so when the doctor told me I had prostate cancer
and said at my age I'd be better
to just live out the last year or two in peace
I told him I knew a trick or two so give me the treatment.
That's five years ago and the side-effects
can lay me up a bit at times,
but I have more hair now because of the zinc,
so it wasn't for nothing – and I'm back down the beach,
walking the same steps from the Barchetta café
onto the sand – nothing like it under your feet –
clean & white, fitting your every movement
like you had been tailored for just this one life.

Cat

They will smell cat on us as we approach
the border crossing. The dogs will growl, drag
their leads. Sniff us till the guards tell us to open
our suitcases. Finding nothing take us
roughly by the arm, murmur back and forth
before throwing us into the back
of vans. We confess to a fondness
of cats, but have been clean for days. Still they
smell cat on us. In this land of dog,
and hordes of native birds, the cats have gone
missing, rounded up and exterminated.
Here the dogs sleep in beds, the birds walk the streets.
They don't like creatures that land on their feet.
Feline sleek, indifferent; too clever to cheat.

www.ingramcontent.com/pod-product-compliance
Lightning Source LLC
Chambersburg PA
CBHW071036080526
44587CB00015B/2636